ELEMENTARY LEVEL

JOHN LANDON

Claws

CW00762239

HEINEMANN ELT

ELEMENTARY LEVEL

Series Editor: John Milne

The Heinemann Elt Guided Readers provide a choice of enjoyable reading material for learners of English. The series is published at five levels – Starter, Beginner, Elementary, Intermediate and Upper. At **Elementary Level**, the control of content and language has the following main features:

Information Control

Stories have straightforward plots and a restricted number of main characters. Information which is vital to the understanding of the story is clearly presented and repeated when necessary. Difficult allusion and metaphor are avoided and cultural backgrounds are made explicit.

Structure Control

Students will meet those grammatical features which they have already been taught in their elementary course of studies. Other grammatical features occasionally occur with which the students may not be so familiar, but their use is made clear through context and reinforcement. This ensures that the reading as well as being enjoyable provides a continual learning situation for the students. Sentences are kept short – a maximum of two clauses in nearly all cases – and within sentences there is a balanced use of simple adverbial and adjectival phrases. Great care is taken with pronoun reference.

Vocabulary Control

At **Elementary Level** there is a limited use of a carefully controlled vocabulary of approximately 1,100 basic words. At the same time, students are given some opportunity to meet new or unfamiliar words in contexts where their meaning is obvious. The meaning of words introduced in this way is reinforced by repetition. Help is also given to the students in the form of vivid illustrations which are closely related to the text.

Contents

1

Dreaming of Mountains

Larry Bakewell was a cook. He studied cookery at college for five years. When he left college, he began to look for a job. He found a job as a cook in a hotel. But he did not like the job and did not stay there for very long. Next, Larry found a job in a busy restaurant. The restaurant was in the centre of the city. He stayed in that job for six months. Then he left. He did not like working in the city.

Larry found other jobs. He worked in a school kitchen for a while, then in a hospital kitchen. But he did not stay in any of these jobs for very long. Sometimes Larry left because he did not like the boss. Sometimes he left because he did not like the work.

It was now the month of May. And Larry had not had a job for four months. He was looking for a job, but he had not found one.

At weekends, Larry did not look for work. Every weekend, he went to the mountains. Larry loved climbing mountains. The mountains were not very far from where he lived. In the mountains he felt free and life was exciting. No one told him what to do. Every day was different. Larry wanted to live in the mountains, but there were no jobs there. Every weekend, Larry had to go back home.

Larry Bakewell was twenty-six. He had short, dark hair and a beard. He liked to wear jeans and sweaters. Larry lived in a small flat with Jack, one of his college friends. The flat was in a large house in the suburbs of the city. Larry and Jack had their own rooms. The walls of Larry's room were covered with pictures of mountains and mountaineers.

There was climbing equipment on the floor.

'Bakewell is a good name for a cook,' Jack often said, and laughed.

'I've got a good name for a cook,' Larry replied. 'But I can't find a job that I like.'

'There must be some exciting jobs somewhere,' Jack said.

'Working in a kitchen isn't exciting.' replied Larry.

It was Monday morning and Larry had to look for a job. He bought a newspaper from the small shop at the corner of the street. It was raining and the streets were wet. People were walking to work in the rain.

I must find a job soon, he thought sadly.

As he walked home, Larry quickly looked through the pages of the newspaper. There were a lot of advertisements for jobs. But Larry did not like any of them. He stopped thinking about the jobs. He began to think about climbing in the mountains.

Suddenly he stopped. He began to read the newspaper more carefully. There was an advertisement on the back page of the newspaper. It was an advertisement for a job. A very unusual job.

This looks interesting! Larry said to himself.

2

Just the Job!

Larry forgot about the mountains. He stood outside the flat and did not open the door. He read the newspaper advertisement again and again.

COOK WANTED

Are you an experienced cook?
Are you 25-30 years old?
Are you strong and healthy?
Have you climbed mountains?

I am taking an expedition to the mountains of northern Afghanistan and we need someone to cook for us. It is a scientific expedition to search for the Toruk, a strange creature that lives in the mountains of Afghanistan. No expedition has seen the Toruk – we will find it.

Apply as soon as possible to:
Professor Max Lugner,
Museum of Natural Science, London

Larry opened the door of the flat.

'Jack,' he shouted. 'Look at this advertisement!'

'What is it?' Jack asked. 'Have you found a job?'

'Look at this,' Larry said again, very excited.

They both read the advertisement together.

'You are an experienced cook,' said Jack. 'And you have climbed mountains.'

'And I'm twenty-six and strong and healthy,' said Larry.

'This is the job for you,' said Jack.

They both read the advertisement again. Then Jack started to laugh.

'But this is silly,' he said. 'No one has seen this creature – the Toruk. They are going to look for something which no one has seen.'

'It isn't silly,' Larry replied. 'It's a job for a cook and it's a job in the mountains. It's the job I've been looking for.'

In the afternoon, Larry went to the library. He did not go to the library often. He did not like libraries. Everyone in the library was sitting quietly and studying hard. But Larry wanted to learn more about the Toruk and about Professor Lugner.

Larry went up to the librarian and asked, 'Where can I find books about animals?'

The librarian pointed to a long shelf on the other side of the library.

'You will find books about animals over there,' the librarian said, and smiled.

Larry looked through the books carefully. Some of them were old and dusty. At last, he found a book with the title *Monsters: Fact or Fiction?*

Perhaps there is something about the Toruk in this book, Larry thought.

Larry opened the book and looked at the titles of the chapters. Each chapter was an article written by a different scientist. And each article was about a strange creature. Larry looked for a chapter about the Toruk.

In chapter five, Larry found what he was looking for.

Larry quickly turned to page 78 and read the first paragraph of Professor Lugner's article.

I have led three expeditions to Afghanistan. Each time we have seen the marks of the Toruk's claws. But we have never seen the Toruk. On the last expedition, the men who saw the claw marks disappeared mysteriously on Mount Kanchen. I believe they were killed by the Toruk. I have seen the claw marks and I am certain that the Toruk lives in the mountains of Afghanistan.

That's strange, Larry thought. All the other men who have seen the claw marks are dead. Only Professor Lugner has seen the marks and is still living, Larry thought to himself.

Larry looked at all the other books on the shelf. He found nothing more about the Toruk.

He looked round the library. Everyone was sitting quietly. They were reading books and studying.

Suddenly Larry decided.

'I'm going to apply for the job,' he said aloud. Everyone stopped reading and looked up at him. Larry ran out of the library. He went to the nearest telephone.

———

Professor Lugner's secretary answered the telephone.

'I'm applying for the job of the cook with Professor Lugner's expedition,' Larry said.

3

The Shadow of the Toruk

A few days later, Larry travelled down to London. He was going to an interview with Professor Lugner. He did not like going to London. The city was crowded and dirty. And he had to wear a suit for the interview. He did not like wearing a suit.

Larry was early. He arrived at the Museum of Natural Science at a quarter past ten. His interview with Professor Lugner was at eleven o'clock.

I'll look around the Museum before the interview, Larry thought to himself.

He went into the large hall of the Museum. In the centre of the hall there were skeletons of huge animals and birds.

Larry looked at the skeletons. He read the notices underneath each of them. Time passed very quickly.

———

*In the centre of the hall there were skeletons of
huge animals and birds.*

Larry looked up at the clock. It was five to eleven.

My goodness! I must hurry, Larry said to himself.

Professor Lugner's office was at the end of the large hall.

'Come in, Mr Bakewell,' the Professor's secretary said politely. 'Professor Lugner will be here in a minute.'

Larry sat down and waited. He saw a door with the Professor's name on it. There were three other people waiting.

Are they applying for the cook's job too? Larry thought. He did not want to look at them. He picked up a newspaper and began to read.

A bell rang.

The secretary said, 'Mr Bakewell, Professor Lugner will see you now.' Larry got up and the secretary showed him into the Professor's room.

It was a large office. On the walls, there were maps and photographs of the other expeditions. But Larry did not see them. He was looking straight in front of him. He was looking at a huge, strange creature – half bird, half animal.

'The Toruk!' said Larry.

The creature was about nine feet tall. Its head touched the ceiling of the room. Larry looked at its large, black eyes and long beak. It had a long beak like a bird, but it did not have wings. Long, hairy arms rested at its sides. It had huge red claws on its hands and feet.

'Those claws have killed four of my friends,' said a voice. Larry had not seen the man who was sitting at the desk beside the creature.

'I am Professor Max Lugner,' the man said.

The Professor was a small man, about forty years old. He stood up and shook Larry's hand. Professor Lugner had thin, grey hair and a small grey moustache.

'The Torulk' said Larry.

The Professor pointed to the creature beside him.

'This is the Toruk,' he said. 'Beautiful, isn't he?'

Larry looked at the Toruk again. He saw that it was made of painted wood.

'How do you know that the Toruk looks like this?' Larry asked the Professor.

'Many years ago, travellers were crossing the mountains into India,' Professor Lugner replied. 'These travellers saw the Toruk. Many of the travellers died. But some of them lived and drew pictures of the Toruk. I have the pictures here.'

The Professor took the old pictures from his desk. Larry looked at the pictures and at the wooden Toruk.

'That was many years ago,' said Larry. 'Has anyone seen the Toruk recently?'

The Professor pointed to a photograph of four men on the wall.

'These four men left the camp one night. They never came back. They saw the Toruk.'

'If the expedition finds the Toruk ...' Larry said.

'If we find him?' said the Professor angrily. 'There is no "if". We shall find him.'

The Professor did not speak for a few moments. He walked around the room. At last he stopped beside a large bookshelf. On the bookshelf there were many books about the Toruk.

'I have written many books about the Toruk,' the Professor said. 'I will write one more book. When I have seen the Toruk myself, I will write my last book. I will tell everybody what it looks like.'

The Professor turned to Larry.

'Now I must ask you some questions,' he said. He asked

Larry about his other jobs and about mountaineering. Larry answered the Professor's questions. But he looked all the time at the wooden Toruk. He looked at the Toruk's cruel red claws.

Then the Professor asked Larry his last question.

'You believe that we will find the Toruk, don't you?'

'Yes, of course,' Larry replied, but he was not sure.

4

Dreams Come True

After the interview, Larry could not sleep very well. Every morning, he got up early. As soon as the postman came he ran to the door. But the postman did not have any letters for him.

At last a letter arrived. The words *Museum of Natural Science* were on the envelope. Larry opened it quickly. He read the first few lines.

Museum of Natural Science
London SW7

5th June, 19..

Dear Mr Bakewell,

We are pleased to offer you the job of cook on our expedition to northern Afghanistan.

Larry did not read any more.

'Jack!' he shouted. 'Jack! I've got it!'

Jack was in the kitchen eating his breakfast.

'Got what?' he asked.

'I've got the job,' said Larry. 'I'm going to Afghanistan.'

'Congratulations, Larry,' Jack said. 'Now sit down and have some breakfast.'

'I can't eat now,' replied Larry. 'I'm too excited.'

'Well, when do you leave?' Jack asked.

'I haven't read all the letter yet,' Larry replied. He began to read the rest of the letter aloud. Jack listened while he was drinking his coffee.

You will attend a meeting for members of the expedition on July 1st. The expedition will leave London by air on September 1st. We will reach Kabul, the capital of Afghanistan, the following day. When we have found guides, we will leave for the mountains. We will begin our search for the Toruk on September 16th.

We will soon see the Toruk.

Yours sincerely,

Max Lugner

MAX LUGNER (Expedition Leader)

'Professor Lugner is sure that he will find the Toruk,' Jack said, when Larry had finished reading the letter.

'Yes,' replied Larry, 'I can't understand him. He has never seen the Toruk. But he is sure that he will find it.'

Jack finished his breakfast. He was in a hurry. He had to run to the station. His train left in five minutes.

I have three weeks before the meeting on the first of July, Larry said to himself. I will find out more about Professor Lugner and the Toruk.

Larry had three questions, and wanted to find the answers to these questions. He wrote the questions in a notebook.

I'll have to go to the library, he thought. He put on his jacket, and walked to the bus-stop.

Larry went to the library every day for the next three weeks. He looked at old newspapers. He read books about Afghanistan. In the evenings, he wrote letters. He wrote to the people who had been with the Professor on the other expeditions.

He found some of the answers to his questions. But he also found other questions that had to be answered.

Perhaps I will find the answers to the other questions when I am in Afghanistan, he thought to himself.

Here is what Larry wrote in his notebook:

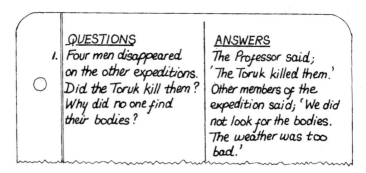

	QUESTIONS	ANSWERS
1.	Four men disappeared on the other expeditions. Did the Toruk kill them? Why did no one find their bodies?	The Professor said; 'The Toruk killed them.' Other members of the expedition said; 'We did not look for the bodies. The weather was too bad.'

2.	Has anyone been on more than one expedition with the Professor?	WHY DOES THE PROFESSOR THINK THE TORUK KILLED THE MEN? No. The Professor always goes with different people. WHY?
3. ○	The Professor says; 'The Toruk has killed many travellers.' Were their bodies found? Did the Toruk kill them?	Many travellers have died in the mountains. The bodies of some of them were found. WERE THESE TRAVELLERS KILLED BY THE TORUK?

5

The First Meeting

On the first of July, Larry travelled to London again. Once more, he walked through the large hall in the Museum of Natural Science. Once more, he looked at the huge skeletons of animals and birds.

The members of the expedition met in a room at the back of the Museum. There were fifteen members: scientists, a doctor, and a quartermaster. The quartermaster looked after the equipment. And, of course, there was the cook.

There were many large boxes and metal cases. The boxes had labels on them: ROPES, FOOD, MEDICAL

SUPPLIES, PHOTOGRAPHIC EQUIPMENT. The quartermaster was bending over the boxes. He was a young man, about the same age as Larry. He was wearing a dark green shirt and sweater.

The quartermaster stood up and spoke to Larry.

'Are you the cook?' he said. 'I'm Greg Chaplin – the quartermaster. How do you do?' They shook hands.

'What was your job before you joined the expedition?' Larry asked Greg.

'I was in the army,' replied Greg. 'But I got tired of life in the army. I wanted to do something different. I applied for the post of quartermaster. And the army let me come on the expedition.'

Larry was pleased.

'I wanted to do something different too,' he told Greg. 'That's why I applied for the job of cook.'

They spoke for a few minutes. Then Greg said, 'We must do some work now.'

He pointed to the large cases marked FOOD.

'These boxes hold all our food,' Greg explained.

Larry looked carefully at the boxes. Underneath the food boxes there was another box. It was a large metal box. It had a label on it which said:

> PROFESSOR LUGNER
> PRIVATE
> DO NOT OPEN

'What's in this box?' Larry asked Greg.

Before Greg could answer, Professor Lugner ran into the room. He was holding a telegram in his hand. Everyone stopped talking.

'Gentlemen,' the Professor said, 'I have received a telegram from Kabul. Wonderful news! Some travellers have seen the Toruk's claw marks. The marks were in the snow near the Mantra Pass. That is four days' journey north of Kabul.'

They all talked excitedly.

The Professor pointed to a large map on the wall.

'We will follow this track through the Afghanistan mountains,' said the Professor, pointing to the map. 'We will start here. This is a village called Khalid. The road ends there. In Khalid, we will find guides who will show us the way. And we will find porters who will carry our boxes and equipment.

Everyone in the room was looking carefully at the map.

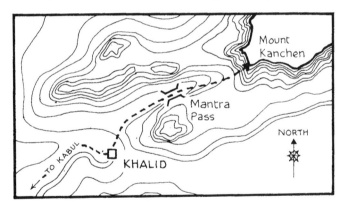

'From Khalid we will climb up to the Mantra Pass,' Professor Lugner went on. 'The expedition will stop at Mount Kanchen, when we have seen the Toruk.'

Larry looked up at the Professor. Larry remembered. The four members of the other expedition had been killed on Mount Kanchen.

19

One of the scientists said, 'I have a question, sir. What is the weather like there?'

The Professor looked unhappy.

'The weather is bad,' he said quietly. 'The weather in September is usually good for expeditions. The bad weather begins in the middle of October. But this year, the bad weather has started early. Heavy snow has already fallen. There is more snow coming.'

'If the weather is bad in Afghanistan, will we wait here in London?' another scientist asked.

'No, we will not wait,' the Professor replied. 'We will fly to Kabul on the first of September.'

6

Ready, Steady … !

When the expedition arrived at Kabul Airport, the sun was shining brightly. But it was not hot. A cold wind was blowing from the mountains in the north. The mountains looked very near. They were cold and unfriendly. There was a lot of snow on the tops of the mountains. And there were large white clouds in the sky above the mountains. More snow was coming.

From Kabul, the expedition travelled in two lorries to the small village of Khalid. Larry and Greg went in one lorry with the boxes and the equipment. The Professor and the scientists went in the second lorry. The road was bad and the journey was very uncomfortable.

The lorries arrived in the village square at Khalid. A large crowd of people came to look at the lorries. It was a crowd of men and boys. The women stayed inside their houses. They watched from the windows and the doorways.

Larry and Greg jumped out of the back of the first lorry. Immediately a crowd of small boys ran up to them. They wanted to see the equipment.

Some of the boys got into the back of the lorry. They tried to open the boxes.

'Get down! Get out of the lorry!' Greg shouted.

Older men from the crowd pulled the boys out of the back of the lorry.

The Professor jumped out of the other lorry and ran up to Greg.

'No one must touch my box!' the Professor shouted angrily.

'It's here,' Greg replied. 'No one has touched it.'

Professor Lugner looked pleased.

'You and the cook go and find porters and guides,' the Professor said to Greg. 'Bring them to me this evening.'

'Let's go,' Greg said to Larry.

Larry and Greg walked along the narrow street. On both sides of the street there were small houses with flat roofs. Thin dogs ran between the houses. Children were playing in the street. They shouted at Larry and Greg. Then they ran away.

Larry and Greg reached the market-place. Men were standing around talking. People were selling vegetables and fruit. Greg went up to some men.

'We want porters and guides for our expedition,' Greg said. He pointed to the mountains. The men understood him. They talked to one another. Larry heard the word, 'Toruk … Toruk'.

One of the men turned to Larry and Greg. He held up his hand like a claw. He said, 'Toruk'. Then he shook his head. The other men shook their heads too. They all walked away.

Larry and Greg went to some more men. The men talked about the Toruk. They then shook their heads and walked away.

'They are frightened,' Larry said to Greg at last.

'They know that the Toruk killed the men on the other expedition,' Greg replied.

Larry and Greg met some young men from another village. These men were looking for work. They also found a mountain guide. He was an old man called Abdul. Abdul knew the mountains well. He had been a guide on another expedition with Professor Lugner. Abdul knew a little English.

'Will you be our guide on this expedition?' Greg asked Abdul. He thought that Abdul would say no. Abdul's face was very brown and his eyes were bright.

'I have been waiting for you,' Abdul said. 'I want to see the Toruk.'

Greg looked at Larry. They were both surprised. Abdul was different from the other villagers. Greg did not ask Abdul any more questions.

Greg and Larry took Abdul and the young men back to Professor Lugner. He was staying with the other members of the expedition in a house in the village. The Professor was pleased to see the young porters. But when he saw Abdul, the Professor became angry.

'Why have you brought this man?' he asked Greg.

'He says he's a guide,' Greg answered. 'He has already been on one of your expeditions.'

'He cannot come with us this time,' the Professor shouted.

'But we must have a guide, sir,' Greg replied. 'He is the only guide who will come with us.'

The Professor looked at the old man. He said nothing for a long time. At last the Professor spoke.

'All right. He can come,' he said.

'I don't understand,' Greg said to Larry. 'We found a good guide. But Professor Lugner didn't want him to come on the expedition.'

'He has been on an expedition before,' Larry replied.

'I know,' said Greg, looking at Larry strangely. 'But that is a good thing, isn't it?'

Larry took his notebook out of his pocket. He showed Greg

his three questions. Then he read aloud, 'Question two: Has anyone been on more than one expedition with the Professor? Answer: No. The Professor always goes with different people. Why?'

'Why is that?' Greg asked.

'I don't know,' Larry replied. 'But we have someone on this expedition who has searched for the Toruk before.'

7

... Go!

There was a lot of work to do before the expedition left Khalid. Greg had to check the equipment carefully. The doctor had to make sure that all the porters were healthy. This was not easy. The porters were afraid of the doctor.

'We are healthy. We do not need a doctor,' they said.

The scientists walked around Khalid and other villages. They asked the villagers about the Toruk.

'Have you seen the Toruk?' they asked. 'What did the Toruk look like?' The villagers did not want to talk about the Toruk. They were frightened.

'If we talk about the Toruk, the Toruk will kill our children,' the villagers told the scientists.

Some of the villagers showed the scientists teeth and hair.

'These come from the Toruk,' they said. 'If we wear these around our necks, the Toruk will not kill us.'

The scientists looked carefully at the teeth and the hair. They were the teeth and hair of horses and cows.

Abdul wanted to leave soon. He knew the mountains.

He understood the weather.

'The clouds are on the tops of the mountains,' Abdul said to Larry. 'That is bad. The wind is coming from the north. There will be more snow.'

Abdul spoke to travellers who came from the mountains.

'The mountain tracks are full of snow,' they said.

'I do not understand your Professor,' Abdul said to Larry. 'He wants to find the Toruk. But he always looks for the Toruk in bad weather.'

Abdul told Larry a lot about the other expedition.

'The weather was very bad then,' Abdul said. 'Many of the men wanted to go back to Khalid.'

'Why didn't you go back?' asked Larry.

'Your Professor wanted to see the Toruk,' Abdul replied quietly. 'Four men died, but your Professor was happy. He saw the Toruk's claw marks. Now he is well-known. He is famous.'

Yes, thought Larry, Professor Lugner got his job at the Museum of Natural Science because of that expedition.

Larry turned to Abdul.

'But why do you want to go on this expedition?' he asked.

Abdul smiled strangely.

'I want to understand your Professor,' he replied.

That evening, Professor Lugner had a meeting with the members of the expedition.

'Everything is ready,' he told them. 'We must start tomorrow. We must climb quickly to the Mantra Pass. Travellers have seen the Toruk's claw marks there.'

Everyone went to bed early that night. They had to leave

at sunrise. But no one slept very well. Larry was thinking about the Toruk.

In the morning, the clouds had gone from the mountain tops. The sky was blue. The tops of the mountains were white with snow. Although it was early, the market-place in Khalid was full of people. They watched quietly.

The porters put the heavy equipment on their backs. They were ready to leave.

As the expedition left the village, the people of Khalid stood quietly. They did not make any noise. Only the dogs barked and ran along behind the expedition. Abdul walked up to Greg and Larry.

'The people of Khalid are sad,' he said. 'They can remember. Your Professor leads men to their deaths.'

Greg laughed. He put his hand on Abdul's shoulder.

'It will be different this time,' he said.

8

Towards the Mantra Pass

The expedition left Khalid quickly and started to go up the mountain paths. The paths were stony and it was not easy to walk on them. But there was no snow. Sometimes the expedition met travellers on the road. They were coming from the north. Their tired horses were carrying heavy goods. They were going to sell their goods in the markets of Kabul.

Professor Lugner talked to the travellers about the Toruk.

'Have you seen the Toruk or the Toruk's claw marks?' the Professor asked them.

The travellers talked quietly to each other before they replied.

'We have not seen the Toruk,' they said at last. But they told the Professor about men who had been killed by the Toruk.

Afterwards, Abdul talked to the travellers and asked them about their journey.

'The weather has been very bad,' Abdul said to Larry. 'The Mantra Pass is full of snow. It is very dangerous.'

'Are you going to tell the Professor?' Larry asked.

'He won't listen,' Abdul replied. 'He does not want to know about the weather. He wants to find the Toruk.'

The expedition climbed higher up the mountain paths. Larry was very happy. He was in the mountains. He had a job which he liked. Every day was different. Larry sometimes thought about his jobs in England.

'I shall never like a job in England again,' he said to Greg one day. Greg thought for a while.

'Why don't you write a diary?' he suggested. 'Why don't

you write down what happens every day? Then you can read about everything when you get back to England.'

'That's a good idea!' Larry replied.

'And later you can write a book about the expedition!' Greg continued. They both laughed.

After supper, Larry went to his tent. He got out his notebook and wrote the date at the top of the page. Then he wrote down what had happened that day.

TUESDAY, SEPTEMBER 19th

This morning we reached the snow. The snow is not very deep here but we have to climb more slowly. The track is steep and dangerous.

One of the porters fell this afternoon. He was carrying Professor Lugner's box. Nothing was broken, but the Professor was very angry.

He did this every night. He made a diary of what happened on the expedition.

WEDNESDAY, SEPTEMBER 20th

We have climbed higher now, and the snow is deeper. There are clouds all around us. Abdul is a very good guide, but he does not like Professor Lugner. He watches the Professor very carefully.

We talk a lot about the Toruk now. Some of the scientists do not believe the stories about the Toruk. They say that there is no Toruk. They say that it does not exist. I am not sure. Perhaps there is a Toruk; perhaps there isn't.

Each night, three men guard the camp. Each man guards the camp for three hours. The guard stays in his tent but he has to keep awake. He has to listen for the Toruk. Greg is guarding the camp tonight.

THURSDAY, SEPTEMBER 21st

Today heavy snow fell. We have not left the camp. The wind is very strong. It is difficult to walk. Some of the scientists went to see the Professor today. They want to go back to Khalid. I do not know why they want to go back. It is dangerous here, but it is very exciting.

FRIDAY, SEPTEMBER 22nd

This morning we all woke up suddenly. There was a loud noise outside the tents. The ground was shaking. The porters began to shout. I looked out of the tent. The air was full of snow. It was falling from the rocks above us.

No one was hurt, but some of the equipment was covered with snow. We have been digging the equipment out of the snow all day.

Tomorrow we will reach the Mantra Pass. Then perhaps we will see the Toruk !

On Friday evening, when Larry finished writing, he was very tired. Everyone was asleep. Larry put out the light. He listened to the wind. He soon fell asleep.

9

Missing, Believed Killed

The next morning Larry woke up early. The porters were already awake. They were moving around and talking outside Larry's tent. Greg was in the same tent as Larry. He was still asleep. Larry lay and listened to the noise of the wind.

What will happen today? he thought to himself.

Suddenly one of the porters began shouting: 'Toruk! Toruk!'

Larry sat up and listened.

'What's that?' asked Greg, waking up suddenly.

'I don't know,' Larry replied. 'I think someone has seen the Toruk.'

Larry and Greg got up as fast as they could. They put on their boots and opened the front of the tent. There was thick cloud all round the tents. It was difficult to see anything clearly.

The other members of the expedition were coming out of their tents. The porters were standing near the Professor's tent. They were waving their arms and shouting. Professor Lugner was with them.

Larry and Greg ran to the Professor. In the snow, not far from the Professor's tent, they saw claw marks.

'It's the Toruk!' shouted Larry.

'The Toruk has been near the camp in the night,' said Greg. 'Look! The marks are clear. There is no new snow on top of them.'

The Professor was bending over one of the claw marks. He was measuring it. He stood up and saw Larry and Greg.

'This is the mark of the Toruk,' he explained to them. 'The Toruk's foot is 36 centimetres wide and 58 centimetres long. The claws are 8 centimetres long.'

He drew a picture of the claw mark in his notebook.

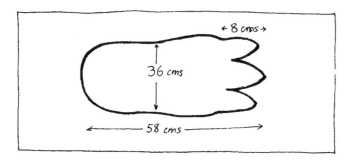

'At last the Toruk has come to us,' the Professor said. 'We will see him soon.'

'I hope I don't meet him first,' Greg said to Larry.

'Why didn't the guard see the Toruk?' Larry asked suddenly.

'I don't know,' replied Greg. 'Where is the guard?'

Soon everyone was asking the same question. The guard was a young scientist called Guy. He had wanted to turn back when the weather became bad.

'Perhaps he has gone back alone,' someone said. 'He wasn't very happy about the expedition.'

'That's impossible,' said another scientist. 'The weather is too bad to travel alone.'

The members of the expedition looked all round the camp. They called out the young man's name. They did not find him. They came back to the place where the claw marks were. Professor Lugner was still there. He had not moved. He was still making notes.

Abdul, the guide, spoke to Larry and Greg.

'Your friend is dead,' he said. 'The Toruk has taken him. You will never see him again.'

'How do you know?' Larry asked Abdul.

'I have seen it happen before,' Abdul replied. 'Four other men died in the same way.'

'Perhaps Guy is still alive somewhere in the mountains,' Greg said. 'We must search for him. We will follow the Toruk's claw marks. Perhaps we will find Guy, and perhaps we will see the Toruk too.'

'That's a good idea,' everyone agreed.

But Professor Lugner was very angry. He walked over to Greg.

'I'm the leader of this expedition,' he said. 'Don't forget that.'

'I'm sorry, sir,' he said to the Professor politely. 'But can't we go out and search for him?'

Professor Lugner looked at everyone standing round him.

'We will not search for him,' he said in a loud voice. 'The Toruk has taken Guy. We can't get him back.'

The men looked at each other in surprise.

'It's foolish to go out and search for him,' the Professor went on. 'The weather is too bad. More men will die.'

The men began to argue with the Professor.

'If we don't look for Guy, we must go back to Khalid immediately,' one man said.

'We will not search,' Professor Lugner replied angrily. 'And we will not go back. I am the leader of this expedition. We will not go back until we have seen the Toruk.'

It was snowing heavily again. The snow was falling on the Toruk's claw marks. It was now difficult to see them clearly. The sky was white. More snow was coming.

'Go back to your tents,' the Professor shouted. 'Bakewell, you make the breakfast. We will stay here until the weather gets better. I will be the guard tonight.'

Everyone went back to their tents. Larry went to make breakfast. Greg and Abdul went with him.

'The same thing. The same thing,' Abdul was saying.

'What do you mean?' Greg asked Abdul.

'We never found the four men who were killed on the last expedition,' Abdul explained. 'We couldn't search for them because the weather was so bad.'

After breakfast, Larry looked again at his notebook. He read what he had written there.

The Professor said: 'The Toruk killed them.' Other members of the expedition said 'We did not look for the bodies. The weather was too bad.'

Why is Professor Lugner sure that the Toruk killed Guy? Larry thought to himself.

10

Professor Lugner on Guard

The snow fell all morning. The men stayed in their tents. They talked about Guy and about the Toruk. Many of the men did not agree with Professor Lugner.

'We must look for Guy,' they said. 'Perhaps he is still alive. We don't know that the Toruk has killed him.'

'The Professor thinks only of the Toruk,' others said. 'He does not care about Guy.'

The porters were also talking about the Toruk. Abdul was very worried.

———

In the afternoon, the snow stopped and the weather was better. It was now possible to look for Guy. Some of the scientists went to talk to Professor Lugner.

'We want to search for Guy,' they said to the Professor. Professor Lugner did not argue.

'All right,' he replied. 'It is very dangerous. But you can go.'

It was difficult to search. They could not see the Toruk's

claw marks. They were covered by the snow. After three hours, the men came back. They had not found anything.

While the men were searching, some of the porters went to see the Professor. Abdul went with them.

'Many of the porters want to go back to Khalid,' Abdul said to Professor Lugner. 'The weather is too bad. We cannot go on. And the porters are afraid of the Toruk.'

The Professor listened. At last, he spoke.

'They can go back,' he said.

Abdul was surprised. He looked at the porters and then he looked at the Professor.

'But who will carry all the equipment?' he asked.

'The expedition will not leave this place,' Professor Lugner replied. 'We will look for the Toruk in the Mantra Pass.'

'But how will you get back to Khalid without the porters?' Abdul asked.

'We do not need porters,' the Professor replied angrily. 'When we go back to Khalid, we will leave the equipment here in the mountains.'

He looked at Abdul. 'You don't want to see the Toruk,' he said. 'But I cannot stop searching for the Toruk now.'

———

There was a strange feeling in the camp that evening.

'I think the Toruk is watching us,' Larry said to Greg.

'And I think it is laughing at us,' Greg replied. 'We haven't seen the Toruk. But I feel it is here.'

Everyone was tired. Larry made a hot meal. The men talked together for a little while. Then they went to bed. Larry could not sleep. He was thinking about the questions in his notebook.

There are not enough answers, he thought to himself.

Larry fell asleep. He dreamt about the Toruk. In his dream he saw the huge animal in Professor Lugner's office in London. It was standing near a tent. The tent was his tent. The Toruk was trying to tear the tent with its sharp claws.

Suddenly Larry woke up. He had heard a noise outside. He looked at his watch. It was half past three.

The Professor is the guard now, Larry thought to himself.

Larry listened. His eyes were wide open. Something was moving slowly near the camp.

Am I still dreaming? Larry thought. Again he heard the sound. It was something large and heavy. It was moving very slowly away from the camp.

Larry did not move. He knew that he was not dreaming now.

Shall I wake Greg up? he thought. He moved towards Greg.

No, he thought. If I wake him up, we will make too much noise.

Larry picked up a large cooking knife. He listened again. The sound was moving further away. He went out of the tent. It was dark outside, but there was some light in the east. Morning was coming. The snow had stopped falling.

Perhaps the Professor has fallen asleep, Larry thought. He went quietly to the Professor's tent. There was no one in the tent. Then he saw the footprints in the snow. They were the Professor's footprints. The footprints were going away from the camp. Larry followed them.

Perhaps the Professor heard the same sound too, Larry thought. Perhaps he needs help.

The Professor's footprints went to some high rocks. Then

36

they stopped. Larry looked around. In the early morning light, he saw a huge claw mark in the snow. Then he saw another. The claw marks were going away from the rocks.

Larry held the knife tightly in his hand.

The Toruk has been near the tents again, he thought to himself. But where is Professor Lugner?

Larry looked up into the rocks.

Perhaps the Professor is hiding in the rocks, he thought.

He climbed up the rocks. He could not see the Professor. Suddenly he stopped. He thought of Guy.

Perhaps the Toruk has killed Professor Lugner too, he said to himself. Larry quickly hid behind some rocks. He did not want the Toruk to see him. He looked out over the snow.

The sky was now brighter. The morning light was shining on the snow. Larry saw the Toruk's claw marks clearly. They went across the snow. At the end of the track of claw marks, Larry saw a figure. He looked from between the rocks. The figure was Professor Lugner.

11

The Professor's Secret

Larry quietly moved over the rocks. He was now nearer to the Professor. He hid behind a rock. The wind was blowing up the mountain towards him. Snow blew from the rocks into his face. His eyes filled with water. It was difficult to see.

Larry watched the Professor for some minutes. Professor Lugner was bending over in the snow. He was carrying something large and heavy. Larry rubbed his eyes and looked again.

37

Larry quickly hid behind some rocks.

I don't believe it! he said to himself. Larry watched the Professor in amazement.

Professor Lugner was holding a huge claw in his hands! He was making the Toruk's claw marks!

As the Professor moved, he was putting the claw over his own footprints. He was hiding his footprints with the marks of the claw. The Toruk's claw marks were left clearly in the snow.

The wind was blowing towards Larry. He heard Professor Lugner speaking. The Professor was talking to himself. As he made each claw mark, he said: 'The Toruk lives! They will see! The Toruk lives!'

Sometimes the Professor looked towards the tents. Larry hid behind the rocks. The Professor did not see him.

Larry watched in silence for many minutes. He felt angry.

The Professor has lied to us, he thought. He wanted to shout. He put his hands to his mouth.

Suddenly a hand came round Larry's neck and covered his mouth. Another hand pulled his knife away from him. Larry fell backwards. Then he saw Greg and Abdul. They were bending over him.

'Be quiet,' Greg said.

Larry pointed to the Professor.

'We know,' said Greg. 'We have seen him too.'

'Your Professor is mad,' said Abdul. 'Everyone in the village knows that he is mad.'

'But why did you follow me?' Larry asked.

'Abdul heard you when you were leaving the camp,' Greg replied. 'He woke me up. We followed you over the rocks.'

'You were in great danger,' Abdul said to Larry. He looked at the ground and went on quietly. 'Your Professor has already killed five men.'

Larry listened in amazement.

'Five men?' he asked. 'Did Professor Lugner kill Guy and the other four men?'

'We can't talk now,' said Greg. 'The Professor will hear us. We must get back to the tents.'

The sun was rising over the mountains. Larry could hear the Professor. He was still saying: 'The Toruk lives! They will see!'

Suddenly Professor Lugner looked up. Greg, Abdul and Larry hid behind the rocks. The Professor stood up and looked around. The huge claw was in his hands.

'He has seen us,' Larry said.

'Keep down behind the rocks,' Greg said.

They lay still. Greg raised his head a little and looked

again. The Professor was bending over with the huge claw.

'It's all right. He hasn't seen us,' Greg said to the others. 'He's finishing his work now.'

The Professor made more claw marks. He was moving towards the rocks.

'He's going to go back to the tents over the rocks,' Greg said to Larry and Abdul. 'We must go.'

They began to climb through the rocks. Larry looked back. He could see the Professor. Professor Lugner had reached the rocks. He was holding the claw in his arms.

Greg, Larry and Abdul went round the tents. They got back before Professor Lugner. They went into their tent and waited.

12

Questions to Answer

Abdul sat with Larry and Greg in their tent. None of them said anything. They waited and listened. Soon they heard Professor Lugner. He was coming back from the other side of the tents.

'He has come back a different way,' Greg said very quietly. 'That's good. He won't see our footprints.'

Professor Lugner went into his tent.

'Now we can talk,' said Greg. 'There are many things to talk about.'

'First, I'll make some coffee,' Larry said to the other two. They all felt thirsty and they wanted time to think.

They drank their coffee slowly.

'Can I ask the first question?' said Larry. 'How did you know that the Professor was making the Toruk's claw marks?'

'Abdul followed the Professor yesterday,' Greg replied. 'He saw the Professor making the claw marks near the tents.'

Abdul went on with the story.

'Guy was the guard,' he said. 'He saw your Professor too. They began to fight. Your Professor killed Guy with the Toruk's claw. I saw it all.'

'But why didn't you tell us this yesterday?' Larry asked Abdul.

'I did not think that anyone would believe me,' Abdul replied.

Larry took out his notebook.

'Now I can answer some of my questions,' he said. 'We know that Professor Lugner killed Guy.'

'And we think that he killed the four men on the other expedition,' said Greg. 'They probably found out what he was doing.'

'So that is why Professor Lugner always has different people on his expeditions,' Larry said.

'You remember that your Professor didn't want me to come on the expedition,' said Abdul. 'He was afraid that I knew too much.'

Larry looked at his third question.

'But many Afghan travellers have seen the Toruk's claw marks too,' Larry said to the others.

'That's true,' said Abdul. 'Your Professor has not made all the claw marks.'

Larry and Greg looked at each other.

'Who made the other claw marks?' Greg asked Abdul.

Abdul smiled and raised his hands in the air.

'I don't know,' he replied. 'Perhaps the Toruk is alive. Perhaps the Toruk does exist.'

Larry put down his notebook.

'So we don't have all the answers,' he said.

There were sounds outside. Some of the scientists were starting to wake up.

'What shall we do now?' Larry asked Greg. 'Someone will find the claw marks soon.'

Greg thought for a while.

'We can't stop the expedition now,' he said. 'I want to find the real Toruk. Perhaps it is alive.'

'But Professor Lugner may kill again,' Larry said.

Abdul looked up.

'Your Professor is mad,' he said to Larry. 'If you say anything, he will kill you.'

Greg turned to Larry.

'All right,' he said. 'We won't tell anyone what we have seen. But we must watch Professor Lugner all the time.'

Larry agreed. It was time for breakfast. He had to make the food for everyone. He got up and went out of the tent. Greg followed him.

'Someone will find the Toruk's claw marks soon,' said Larry.

'Perhaps it will be Professor Lugner,' Greg replied. 'He doesn't want the scientists to see his footprints near the Toruk's claw marks.'

'The Professor will find my footprints in the snow!' Larry said to Greg. 'He will know that I saw him last night.'

'Come on,' Larry said. 'We must hurry. We must find the Toruk's claw marks before the Professor does.'

They quickly ran towards the rocks. As they went, they

ran over Larry's footprints.

'The Professor won't see your footprints now,' Greg said to Larry. They came to the rocks and found the claw marks and Professor Lugner's last footprint. They stopped and shouted: 'Claw marks! The Toruk!'

Some of the scientists ran out of their tents. They came up to Larry and Greg and looked at the claw marks. Everyone was excited. Professor Lugner came up to them. He looked worried.

He knows that we have seen his footprint beside the Toruk's claw mark, Larry thought to himself. He wanted to get here first.

Greg began to talk to some of the scientists. He wanted the Professor to hear him.

'Professor Lugner has already seen the claw marks,' he said. 'He saw them last night. Look, here are his footprints!'

Professor Lugner looked surprised. He spoke slowly.

'Yes, I saw them last night,' he said. 'I was going to tell you all after breakfast. I did not want to frighten the porters again.'

Greg walked up to the Professor and shook his hand.

'Congratulations, sir,' he said. 'You must be very happy. We are sure to see the Toruk soon.'

'That is my dream,' he said. 'Many people say that the Toruk does not exist. But now we know that he does.' He began to speak more loudly.

'The Toruk lives!' he went on. 'They will see! He is alive.'

Larry looked at Greg. They remembered those words. Greg spoke again to the Professor.

'Bakewell and I want to guard the camp tonight, sir,' he said. 'We want to see the Toruk.'

Professor Lugner agreed.

'Who will be the other guard?' Professor Lugner asked the scientists. 'It is very dangerous. The Toruk has already taken one man.'

Abdul came to the front.

'I will be the other guard,' he said.

The Professor looked at him and said nothing.

'If Abdul is the other guard, the porters will feel happier,' one of the scientists said. The others agreed.

The Professor looked down at the Toruk's claw marks, and then at Abdul. Abdul smiled.

'All right. Abdul will be the other guard,' the Professor said. Then he walked away.

13

Noises in the Night

Larry cooked breakfast. Everyone ate together. But Professor Lugner was not there. He stayed in his tent. Everyone was talking about the Toruk. Larry, Greg and Abdul did not say anything about what they had seen.

After breakfast, Professor Lugner talked to the men. Together they made plans for their search. One of the scientists spoke about the weather.

'The weather will be very good today,' he said. 'But it is going to get bad soon. There will be strong winds and more heavy snow.'

'We haven't much time,' Professor Lugner said to the members of the expedition. 'Today, some of us will search above those rocks. The others will come with me. We will search around Mount Kanchen.'

Larry and Greg went with Professor Lugner. They watched him carefully. They started to climb Mount Kanchen. It was very steep and they climbed slowly. The sky was blue. They could see other mountains far away to the north.

They searched all day. They found nothing. They returned to the tents in the early evening. The others were already there. They had not seen the Toruk or its claw marks.

The sun set behind the mountains. It became dark. Larry was the first guard. While the others slept, he sat in his tent.

'If you hear the Professor, wake me up,' Greg said to Larry. 'Bad weather is coming and he will probably go out again tonight.'

Larry wrote in his diary as usual, and listened.

What am I listening for? he asked himself. Am I listening for Lugner? Or am I listening for the real Toruk?

Larry was very tired after the climbing and the walking. It was difficult to keep awake. Sometimes he fell asleep for a moment, but he soon woke up. Later in the night, he made some coffee.

At eleven o'clock, Larry heard noises outside. Professor Lugner was coming out of his tent. He came towards Larry's tent and stopped. He called Larry's name quietly.

'Bakewell, Bakewell, are you awake?' he asked.

Larry suddenly felt very frightened.

Does he know that I saw him making the claw marks? he thought. Does he want to kill me now?

Larry did not speak. The Professor went away. He went back to his own tent. Larry listened. He heard the Professor opening a box. Then he heard the box closing again.

So that's where he keeps the claw, Larry thought to himself. It's in his metal box. Now I know why he watched the box so carefully.

Larry moved quietly to the door of his tent and watched carefully. He saw Professor Lugner coming out of his tent. The Professor walked slowly away from the camp. When he reached the rocks, he began to make the claw marks.

Larry woke Greg up. They went out of the tent together and climbed the rocks. The Professor was going a different way this time. He climbed a small hill of snow towards the north. Larry and Greg could not see him now.

'Shall we follow him?' Larry asked Greg.

'No,' Greg replied. 'We mustn't leave our footprints in the snow. We must stay here. If anyone follows the Professor we must stop them.'

They sat and listened for sounds from the tents. They listened for the Professor. Everything was quiet.

Larry and Greg waited for half an hour.

'I'm getting cold,' Larry said to Greg.

'So am I,' said Greg. 'We'll go back to the tents soon. We can listen from our tent.'

They climbed back towards the camp. Suddenly, in the

north, they heard a terrible scream. Larry and Greg stopped and listened. Everything was silent. There were no more sounds.

14

A Meeting at Midnight

The silence was frightening. The sound of the wind had stopped. Larry and Greg stood still. They did not know what to do.

'What's happened?' Larry asked Greg.

'I don't know,' Greg replied. 'I think something has happened to the Professor.'

'We must go back to the tents,' Larry said. 'We will need help.'

Greg did not reply. He was listening for another sound.

'Perhaps we will hear something,' Greg said. 'Then we will know that the Professor is still alive.'

They stood silently and listened. Then Larry and Greg heard a sound.

'The Professor's alive,' Larry said. He was pleased. He did not like Professor Lugner, but he did not want him to die.

'Be quiet!' said Greg. 'Listen!'

There were more sounds. They were the sounds of something large and heavy. The sounds were moving away from Greg and Larry.

'It's the Professor,' said Larry. 'He is all right. He is making the Toruk's claw marks again.'

Greg was not sure.

'But why did he scream so loudly?' he asked. 'We must go and find out.'

The sounds were moving away. They could not hear them clearly.

'The Professor is moving very quickly,' Larry said.

Larry and Greg climbed down from the rocks. They walked across the snow.

'What about our footprints?' Larry asked.

'It doesn't matter now,' Greg replied. 'If the Professor is hurt, we will have to get help. Then everyone will know what he has been doing.'

Larry and Greg found the Toruk's claw marks. They both climbed up hill. They reached the top and looked over. The other side of the hill was steep. Larry and Greg could see the track of the claw marks. The track went behind some rocks.

'The Professor is somewhere behind those rocks,' Greg said.

Larry went over the top of the hill first. The snow was deep. His legs went into it. It was difficult to walk.

'We must stay near the rocks,' he said to Greg. 'The snow isn't so deep there, and the rocks will hide us.'

They climbed up the rocks. Larry looked over a rock and saw the Professor. He was bending over in the snow.

Greg stood beside Larry. They both watched the Professor.

'He is looking away from us,' Larry said. 'And he isn't moving.'

They waited but the Professor did not move.

'Shall we go nearer to him?' Larry asked Greg.

'We'll go very slowly and very quietly,' Greg replied. 'We don't want him to hear us.'

Larry and Greg moved forward slowly. They moved nearer to the Professor. The Professor was not moving. Greg stopped and spoke quietly to Larry.

'You go to the left,' he said. 'I will move to the right. When I put up my hand, call Professor Lugner's name. He'll turn and look at you. Then I'll run and jump on him.'

'I understand,' Larry said.

Larry moved through the snow to the left. Greg went to the right. He put up his hand. He was ready to run towards Professor Lugner. Larry called Professor Lugner's name.

'Professor Lugner! Professor Lugner!' The Professor did not move. Greg looked at Larry. Larry called again. This time he called more loudly.

'Come on!' Greg shouted.

They both ran towards Professor Lugner. He was dead. His body was bending over in the snow.

'Look at the snow,' Larry said to Greg. For the first time they saw that the snow was red with blood.

Larry touched Professor Lugner's body. It fell down on the snow.

'Claw marks!' said Larry.

The front of Professor Lugner's body was covered in blood. His clothes were torn. Huge claws had torn open his face and arms.

Greg looked around.

'Where is the Toruk's claw that the Professor was carrying?' he asked.

'It's here in the snow,' Larry replied. 'There's no blood on it!'

'Greg, look!' Larry shouted.

He was pointing down the hill away from the Professor's body.

The front of Professor Lugner's body was covered in blood.
His clothes were torn.

'The Toruk's claw marks go on across the snow!' he said. A track of claw marks went down the side of the mountain. Larry looked at Greg. 'The Toruk does exist,' he said.

15

A Job for Larry

The members of the expedition went back to Kabul. They got on the plane for London. At London Airport, newspaper and television reporters were waiting for them. The reporters asked many questions about the expedition. And they took lots of photographs.

Daily Messenger

LONDON, SUNDAY, 08 .MORSS- 1900

DOES THE TORUK EXIST?

LARRY BAKEWELL TELLS HIS AMAZING STORY

DOUBLY FOR OLD BOWNRO YEMB MF USAGBNHEN XBWA?
GRSTY QIX KILABOS QOECITI WARIET PERFORMOKS THERE
OOMRMZ OFDIAYB OTH ECOXOM SO ITX WAE EQXEI NONGRST
ZPRSNED YXOPX D BABI IN THE JKMQZI ISFX FOR USEBEREN
YMBO IZA WAEB WHFIS EKYYSTV AMABU LNQUATUM COM MAETUA.

Larry was famous. His picture was on the front page of every newspaper in the country.

Larry was very busy. Everyone wanted to know about the

Toruk and Professor Lugner. Larry had to go to meetings. He had to talk to famous scientists. There was no time to look for jobs now.

Two weeks after they came back, Larry and Greg were on television. They were asked more questions about the Toruk.

'Why did Professor Lugner make the Toruk's claw marks?' they were asked.

'The Toruk had made the Professor famous,' Larry replied. 'He wanted to show everyone that the Toruk exists.'

'And he did show everyone,' Greg added.

After the television interview, Larry was saying goodbye to Greg.

'What are you going to do now, Greg?' he asked.

'I'm going back to the army,' Greg replied. 'And what are you going to do Larry?'

'I don't know,' Larry replied.

'Why don't you write a book?' Greg said. 'You can call it *In Search of the Toruk*.'

Larry laughed.

That night, Larry got out his diary. He began to read it again. Then he started to write. He did not go to bed. He wrote all night.

———

A year later, Larry's book was on sale in the bookshops. On the front was a picture of the Toruk. It was the wooden Toruk which stood in Professor Lugner's room. Many people bought the book.

One day, Greg was walking through the centre of London. He walked past a bookshop. He saw a notice in the window.

There were lots of people inside the shop. They had all
bought a copy of Larry's book. They were waiting for Larry
to sign their copies. Greg bought a copy too. He stood and
waited.

'Next person, please,' Larry said.

He did not see Greg. He did not look up. He wrote in
Greg's book.

With best wishes

Larry Bakewell

'What are you going to do now?' Greg asked Larry.

Larry knew Greg's voice immediately. He looked up and
laughed.

'I'm going on an expedition to look for the Toruk,' said Larry. 'We will find the Toruk this time. I am sure.'

'I've heard that before,' Greg said to Larry. 'May I apply for the post of quartermaster?'

POINTS
FOR
UNDERSTANDING

Points for Understanding

1

1 What did Larry Bakewell study at college?
2 Why did Larry not stay for long in any job?
3 Where was life exciting for Larry?
4 What was Larry looking at in the pages of the newspaper?

2

1 Larry read the newspaper advertisement again and again.
    (a) What job was advertised?
    (b) Where was the expedition going?
    (c) What was the expedition going to look for?
    (d) What kind of experience was necessary?
2 Why did Jack think the advertisement was silly?
3 'It isn't silly,' Larry replied. Why did Larry think the advertisement was not silly?
4 Larry found a book in the library. The book had a chapter in it called *The Toruk's Claws.*
    (a) Who had written the chapter?
    (b) Where had Larry seen his name before?
    (c) What had happened to the men who had seen the Toruk's claw marks?
5 What did Larry decide to do?

3

1 There were many things in Professor Lugner's office, but Larry did not see them.
    (a) What was Larry looking at?
    (b) What did it have on its hands and feet?
    (c) What was it made of?
2 How many men had been killed on another expedition?
3 'If the expedition finds the Toruk …' said Larry. What did Professor Lugner say angrily?

4 'You believe that we will find the Toruk, don't you?' the Professor asked Larry.
    (a)   What did Larry reply?
    (b)   Was Larry telling the truth?

4

1 Larry received a letter from Professor Lugner.
    (a)   What did the first few lines of the letter tell Larry?
    (b)   When was the meeting of the expedition?
    (c)   When would the expedition leave London?
    (d)   When would they begin their search for the Toruk?
2 What were the first two questions which Larry wrote in his notebook?
3 Larry found some answers to his questions. But he also found some other questions. What were these other questions?

5

1 At the meeting of the expedition, Larry met Greg Chaplin.
    (a)   What was Greg's job on the expedition?
    (b)   Why had Greg joined the expedition?
    (c)   Why was Larry pleased?
2 There was a large box underneath the food boxes. What was written on the label on this box?
3 Where had some travellers seen the Toruk's claw marks?
4 In what village was the expedition going to find guides?
5 The expedition will finish at Mount Kanchen. What did Larry remember about Mount Kanchen?
6 A scientist asked Professor Lugner: 'If the weather is bad, will we wait here in London?' What was the Professor's reply?

6

1 What did Professor Lugner shout angrily when some boys jumped onto the back of the first lorry?
2 'They are frightened,' Larry said to Greg at last.
    (a)   Who were frightened?
    (b)   What did Greg think was the reason for their fear?

3 'I have been waiting for you,' Abdul said to Greg and Larry.
    (a)   Who was Abdul?
    (b)   What was unusual about him?
    (c)   Why did Abdul want to come on the expedition?
4 Larry read Question Two aloud to Greg. What was the second question?
5 What did Larry say was the difference between this expedition and the other expeditions?

7

1 Some of the villagers showed the scientists teeth and hair. Had these teeth and hair come from the Toruk?
2 'I do not understand your Professor,' Abdul said to Larry. What did Abdul not understand?
3 'Why do you want to go on this expedition?' Larry asked Abdul. What was Abdul's reply?
4 As the expedition left Khalid, the villagers did not make any noise. What did Abdul say was the reason for this?

8

1 What did Larry start to do every night?
2 Why was Professor Lugner angry when one of the porters fell?
3 How many men guarded the tents each night? How long did each man guard for?
4 Why did some of the scientists want to go back to Khalid?

9

1 What marks were in the snow in the morning?
2 Who had been on guard? Where was he?
3 Why did Abdul say: 'Your friend is dead.'?
4 'That's a good idea,' everyone agreed.
    (a)   What was the idea?
    (b)   What did Professor Lugner think of the idea?
5 Who would be the guard that night?

6   'The same thing. The same thing,' Abdul was saying. What did Abdul mean by 'the same thing'?
7   What had Larry written on his notebook before the expedition started?

10

1   The men who went to look for Guy would not see the Toruk's claw marks. Why not?
2   'We do not need porters,' said Professor Lugner.
    (a)   Why did many of the porters want to go back to Khalid?
    (b)   Why would they not need porters to carry the equipment up the Mantra Pass?
    (c)   Why would they not need porters to carry the equipment back to Khalid?
3   Why did Larry wake up suddenly?
4   Larry went to the Professor's tent. What did he find there?
5   Whose footsteps did Larry follow?
6   What did Larry see in the snow going away from the rocks?
7   Why did Larry hide behind some rocks?
8   Who did Larry see at the end of the track of claw marks?

11

1   Larry watched Professor Lugner for some minutes.
    (a)   What was the Professor doing?
    (b)   What was the Professor saying?
2   'You were in great danger,' Abdul said to Larry. Why had Larry been in great danger?
3   How did Professor Lugner go back to the tents?

12

1   Why had Professor Lugner killed Guy?
2   'But why didn't you tell us this yesterday?' Larry asked Abdul. What was Abdul's reply?
3   Why had Professor Lugner not wanted Abdul to come on the expedition?

4 'Who made the other claw marks?' Greg asked Abdul.
    (a)   What other claw marks had been seen?
    (b)   What was Abdul's reply to Greg's question?
5 What did Larry, Greg and Abdul decide to do?
6 Why did Greg want to be the first to find the claw marks?
7 Why did Greg say: 'Professor Lugner has already seen the claw marks.'?
8 Who would be the three guards the next night?

13

1 What am I listening for? Larry asked himself. Why was Larry not sure about what he was listening for?
2 Larry heard the Professor opening his box. What did the Professor keep in the locked box?
3 What did Larry and Greg hear as they were climbing back towards the tents?

14

1 Larry and Greg heard the sounds of something large and heavy.
    (a)   Who did Larry think was making the sounds?
    (b)   Did Greg agree with Larry?
2 What happened when Larry touched Professor Lugner?
3 What did they see on the snow?
4 What was strange about the wooden claw?
5 Why did Larry say to Greg: 'The Toruk does exist.' ?

15

1 Larry had no time to look for jobs. What was he busy doing?
2 What did Greg tell Larry he should do?
3 'What are you going to do now?' Greg asked Larry.
    (a)   Where were they?
    (b)   What was Larry's reply?
    (c)   What did Greg want to do?

ELEMENTARY LEVEL

Road to Nowhere *by John Milne*
The Black Cat *by John Milne*
Don't Tell Me What To Do *by Michael Hardcastle*
The Runaways *by Victor Canning*
The Red Pony *by John Steinbeck*
The Goalkeeper's Revenge and Other Stories *by Bill Naughton*
The Stranger *by Norman Whitney*
The Promise *by R. L. Scott-Buccleuch*
The Man With No Name *by Evelyn Davies and Peter Town*
The Cleverest Person in the World *by Norman Whitney*
Claws *by John Landon*
Z for Zachariah *by Robert C. O'Brien*
Tales of Horror *by Bram Stoker*
Frankenstein *by Mary Shelley*
Silver Blaze and Other Stories *by Sir Arthur Conan Doyle*
Tales of Ten Worlds *by Arthur C. Clarke*
The Boy Who Was Afraid *by Armstrong Sperry*
Room 13 and Other Ghost Stories *by M. R. James*
The Narrow Path *by Francis Selormey*
The Woman in Black *by Susan Hill*

For further information on the full selection of
Readers at all five levels in the series, please refer
to the Heinemann Readers catalogue.

Macmillan Heinemann English Language Teaching, Oxford

A division of Macmillan Publishers Limited

Companies and representatives throughout the world

ISBN 0 435 272188 1

Heinemann is a registered trademark of Reed Educational & Professional Publishing Limited

Illustrated by Bob Harvey
Typography by Adrian Hodgkins
Cover by Graham Humphreys and Threefold Design
Typeset in 11.5/14.5 pt Goudy
by Joshua Associates Ltd, Oxford
Printed and bound in Great Britain by Fine Print (Services) Ltd., Oxford

98 99 00 01 02 03 04 05 06